SONG OF SONGS

Song of Songs

of Solomon

Translated by

Christopher Kelly, Ph. D.

Song of Songs of Solomon: A New Translation
©2015 Christopher Kelly
All Rights Reserved

Now Experience Books
Los Angeles, California
songofsongs@thenowexperience.com

ISBN 978-0-9861230-6-1

Designed by Christopher Kelly

for Jessica, my love

My deepest gratitude and love to my mother, Brigit Pegeen Kelly, for her inspiration, encouragement and help. She is the greatest poet I know.

Unending appreciation to Jessica Graham for her unending support.

And much thanks to Will Hickman, my editor and friend.

CONTENTS

PART I

Night One

Night Two
My Lover Calls {2:8-2:17}

Night Three

INTRODUCTION

The Song of Songs is a profoundly mysterious text.

It holds a respected and protected place in the central religious text of western civilization. It is a central poem to both Christian and Jewish mystics. It was the most copied book of the Bible by monks of the middle ages, as well as being the single most translated section of the Bible. Akiva Ben Joseph said,

> "All of eternity is not worthy as the day on which the Song of Songs was given to Israel, for all the Writings are holy, but the Song of Songs is the Holy of Holies!"

For all this, the Song never overtly addresses religion, or God, or spirituality, or morality. It focuses, instead, on love and love-making. It talks of passion and romance, of arousal and flirtation, of female and male beauty, and then again of love and more love.

For some, the Song is a collection of traditional love songs or wedding songs only loosely related. For others, it forms a coherent story about a girl and her lover/spouse. For others it is religious or mystical allegory. For many others, narrative and meaning are beside the point; to them, the poem has an intricate and sophisticated thematic and lyrical structure. And for each of these theories, there are dozens of competing sub-theories and combinations of theories. Indeed, the theories of *when* it was written (or collected) cover a thousand years.

So what is the Song? Is it an erotic love poem? A mystical treatise? An ancient Romeo and Juliet? An intricate work of structural poetry? An allegory for Christ, for the Church, for the history of Israel?

The primary goal of the present translation is to explore a structural theory of the Songs, one that I find both fascinating and compelling. It is the theory that the Song of Songs has a *chiastic* or *ring* structure. I first encountered this theory in a wonderful article by J Cheryl Exum, "A Literary and Structural Analysis of the Song of Songs." Many others have explored this theory by this point, but none of which I am aware have attempted a translation using the chiastic structural theory as the guide.

Chiastic or ring structure is a pattern of repetition within a poem. The repetition can be of ideas or words or actions. Take a poem with three main ideas. A chiastic or ring structure could be laid out: ABCB'A'. The C part of the poem is within the B Ring which itself is within the A Ring. More simply, chiasm is the repetition of a series of ideas or words or actions in *reverse* order.

Here is a simple example from within the Song:

> *Let me see your face.*
> *Let me hear your voice.*
> *For your voice is delicious.*
> *And your face is lovely.*

Face = A
Voice = B

The pattern here is ABBA. There are a number of other small examples in the Song. This chiastic structure is common in the Bible, in ancient Hebrew poetry, and other epic poetry of the ancient world.

My translation makes clear that the poem is built of two interlocking macrostructures. I call them "cycles" and "circles." The cycles (also referred to as "Nights") are *narrative in nature*. They will be explained in the next section. The circles are *chiastic in nature* and will be explained in the section after that.

Often, those who see the Song as chiastic are thought to be in opposition to those who see the Song as a clear narrative. I believe that both forms are present and significant. Indeed, it is the overlapping and intertwining of these two major forms that gives the Song its intricate structure. I suggest that understanding the narrative shape of the poem enhances one's understanding of the ring shape and *vice versa*.

The Narrative Structure

I have divided the Song into seven longer poems, "Nights." The Song begins on Night One and ends on Night Seven.

Each Night opens with a call to, or arrival of, one lover. Implicit then is that each Night begins with the lovers apart. Each of the Nights end with either some suggestion of lovemaking or some suggestion of being together and needing to part soon. Three of the Nights end with an explicit reference to the coming of dawn. The poem, then, is made up of seven trysts.

Night Two sets the pattern most clearly. It begins with the lover *arriving:*

> Hark! Hear my lover.
> Look! See he comes now.

Then he makes a request:

Come arise, my darling.
My lovely one, come away.

The Night ends with the lovers together:

> My lover is mine and I am my lover's!

And the lover having to flee because the dawn is coming:

> Now, before the day breathes
> And the shadows flee,
> Turn from me and be, my lover,
> As a gazelle or a wild roe,
> On the cleft and jagged mountains.

Some variation of this pattern helps us lay out the remaining Nights. They begin with the lovers in some form of separation either with *arriving, seeking* or *calling/requesting* – and end with some form of coming together *love-making* or *dawn forcing them to separate again.* The Nights always end with one of or part of one of the many refrains in the poem. The strategy in solving the narrative mystery, then, is to look for clear endings of Nights followed by clear beginnings of Nights.

Night One begins with the girl *requesting* her lover to bring them together:

> Haste me away with you, my king
> And bring me with you to the king's chambers.

A few stanzas later, she continues with this, trying to arrange a meeting:

> Tell me, my soul's chosen lover,
> Where will you desire to graze today?

Night One ends with *love-making/togetherness:*

His left hand under my head,
His right hand embraces me.

And the refrain:

I beg of you, swear it, Daughters of Jerusalem,
By the gazelles and the does of the wild
Do not disturb, do not bestir our loving
Until our love is satisfied.

Night One's ending is followed by the clear *calling* start of
Night Two (above).

Night Three begins with her seeking her lover:

And I sought my soul's chosen love.
I sought but found him not.

And ends with a variation on the ending of Night Two:

*Now before the day breathes
And the shadows flee,
I will hie me to the mountain of myrrh
And to the hill of frankincense!*

Night Four begins with the lover *requesting* the girl to *come:*

*From the ranges of Lebanon, bride,
From the ranges of Lebanon, come.
Descend from the peak of Amana*

Night Four ends with the lovemaking stanza:

*I have come into my garden, my sister, my bride.
Not only have I gathered my myrrh, but also my spice.
Not only have I eaten my honeycomb, but also my honey.*

Not only have I drunk my wine, but also my milk.

Night Four's ending is clearly delineated by the beginning of Night Five.

Night Five begins with the lover *requesting:*

> Open to me, my sister, my darling,
> My dove, my perfect one.

And follows that with the girl s*eeking:*

> I sought but found him not.
> I called but he answered not.

Night Five has an extended ending. It begins with lines referencing both the ending of Night Four and Night Two.

> My lover has come down to his garden
> To the beds of spices.
> He will graze in the garden
> and gather the wild scarlet.
> I am my lover's and my lover is mine!
> He grazes through the wild scarlet.

As in the end of Night Four he "comes into the garden" and as in the end of Night Two, he "grazes" in the "wild scarlet." She utters again the chiastic phrase "I am my lover's and my lover is mine." See the ABBA structure?

Following this first ending, is a long *wasf* (poem of praise) to his lover. This *wasf* is also followed with an allusion to lovemaking to end Night Five. Once again he comes to the garden:

I'd come to the garden of walnut trees

And then:

> Before I was aware, my soul's desire had set me
> On the pillowed throne-bed with my prince.

Night Six begins with a *call:*

> Turn, turn back, O flawless one, Shulammite!
> Turn, turn back, that we may study you!

And ends with yet another call back to the end of Night Two:

> Flowing to my lover smoothly,
> Flowing onto scarlet lips.
> I am my lover's and for me is his passion.

Night Six's ending is made more clear by the beginning of Night Seven, yet another *call* and *request:*

> Come, lover, let's to the fields
> Let's lie all night among the henna
> Let's be off early to the vineyards

Night Seven ends the whole poem with yet another request to hurry away before the dawn rises, calling back to the ending of Night Two and Night Three.

> Haste you away, lover...
> And be as a gazelle or a wild roe
> On all the mountains of spices...

To recap:

Night	Beginning (seeking/coming together)	Ending (together/ needing to part)
One	Haste me away with you, my king And bring me with you to the king's chambers.	His left hand under my head, His right hand embraces me. I beg of you, swear it, Daughters of Jerusalem, By the gazelles and the does of the wild Do not disturb, do not bestir our loving Until our love is satisfied.
Two	Hark! Hear my lover. Look! See he comes now.... *Come arise, my darling. My lovely one, come away*	My lover is mine and I am my lover's! Now, before the day breathes And the shadows flee, Turn from me and be, my lover, As a gazelle or a wild roe, On the cleft and jagged mountains.
Three	And I sought my soul's chosen love. I sought but found him not.	*Now before the day breathes And the shadows flee, I will hie me to the mountain of myrrh And to the hill of frankincense!*
Four	*From the ranges of Lebanon, bride, From the ranges of Lebanon, come. Descend from the peak of Amana*	*I have come into my garden, my sister, my bride. Not only have I gathered my myrrh, but also my spice. Not only have I eaten my honeycomb, but also my honey. Not only have I drunk my wine, but also my milk.*
Five	*Open to me, my sister, my darling, My dove, my perfect one....* I sought but found him not. I called but he answered not.	My lover has come down to his garden To the beds of spices. He will graze in the garden and gather the wild scarlet. I am my lover's and my lover is mine! He grazes through the wild scarlet.... *I'd come to the garden of walnut trees....* Before I was aware, my soul's desire had set me On the pillowed throne-bed with my prince.
Six	Turn, turn back, O flawless one, Shulammite! Turn, turn back, that we may study you!	Flowing to my lover smoothly, Flowing onto scarlet lips. I am my lover's and for me is his passion.
Seven	Come, lover, let's to the fields Let's lie all night among the henna Let's be off early to the vineyards	Haste you away, lover... And be as a gazelle or a wild roe On all the mountains of spices...

Once this structure is in place, the narrative arc of the poem becomes less mysterious. First and foremost, the poem is an exploration of the energy, excitement, pain and drama of falling in love. The constant coming together, the eagerness to be with each other, the delight and heightened emotion when they are together, the dread of being separated.

More specifically, it is about a girl from the vineyards and a shepherd boy. They steal love in the forests and the fields. They play at being a king and a queen. There is flirtation and praise. There is touch and love-making. There is aching for the lover who is not near. There is the danger of being caught. One does not need to know the details of each event to recognize these events, nor to feel the rich evocation of such young love.

The Night structure also makes it clear that the narrative of the poem arcs in a clear direction: the love intensifies, the fantasies grow more involved and elaborate, and the dangers of being caught become more real. The use of repetition and, more importantly, the variations within the repetitions bring out the growth and change of our characters and their relationship.

Most significantly, our central character matures and develops. In the beginning, she says "My vineyard own did not I keep." By the end, "My vineyard own I keep before me now." In context, both suggest a girl that is accepting of her sexuality, but the difference between the two is significant. The first phrase evokes a young girl letting herself be stolen while the second is a girl taking ownership of her sexuality. Compare for yourself Night One and Night Seven. Note specifically the subtle and important change in how she talks to her brothers, and what she says to the Daughters of Jerusalem. Note how she calls to her lover to begin Night Seven rather than the other way around. Note how she interrupts her lover in mid-thought at the end of the poem. Note that at the beginning of the poem, all the women want her king, but at the end of the poem, all his companions attend to *her*. Reversal after reversal.

I have broken the poem into two parts. This is both to emphasize the chiastic structure (which I will discuss in a moment) and to note a dramatic change of tone and intensity that happens at the beginning of Part II (Night Five). Night Five repeats several lines and events that happened in earlier Nights, but it is by far the most detailed narratively and the most explicit sexually. It is as if the whole poem had been playing around the subject until this moment.

Night Five starts with the opening request and then follows with some of the most sensual language in the poem:

> The hard of his hand through the hole
> in the door thrust my love.
> My innermost loins moved at his cause.

The girl then repeats the "I sought but found him not" construction, but the context is entirely different. Whereas the first version of this couplet referred to her mere longing to be with her lover, this second comes after his sudden departure ("he'd turned and fled"). She is now seeking a boy who has left her. This is a new stage in their relationship, and though we can't know what really happened, we all know this moment in the process of falling in love: the first trouble, the first challenge, the terror of opening up to someone and then being rejected. This drama is further intensified or exemplified when she is beaten by the watchmen for being out at night. These are the same watchmen who earlier she had gone to for help, looking for her lover. The poem has turned darker.

Once again, she appeals to the Daughters of Jerusalem, but this time, she says:

I beg of you to swear it, Daughters of Jerusalem,
If you find my lover, what will you tell him?
Do not tell him I am faint with desire.

Again, we see how variation within the repetition serves to show the development of the story. Most of the elements of Night Five call back to earlier parts of the poem, sometimes repeating them almost word for word. Each is varied either by context, wording, or construction, and each of these variations tells us how things have changed in the relationship.

The Chiastic Structure

This semi-narrative organization is only one level of structure in the poem. Once the poem is broken into its seven parts, a natural chiastic ordering presents itself: ABCDC'B'A'.

Night One	Night Two	Night Three	Night Four	Night Five	Night Six	Night Seven
A	B	C	D	C'	B'	A'

Does the content of these Nights support this ordering?

Night One and Night Seven form the outer ring. It is impossible to avoid the similarities between these two portions of the Song. Not only are there many resonances between these two outer poems, but, fascinatingly, *the structure of the first poem is the reverse of the structure of the last poem*. The elements that appear first in the Song of Songs also appear last. What this means is that the AA' ring of the poem is actually constructed of several small rings.

Here I note the six strongest elements of repetition, putting the elements of Night Seven in *reverse* order.

NIGHT ONE **Beginning**	NIGHT SEVEN **Ending**
Haste me away with you....	Haste you away....
Pavilions of Solomon....	Solomon had a Vineyard....
My vineyard own I did not keep....	My vineyard own I keep before me know
Brothers were incensed with me....	Brothers: "We have a younger sister"...
Like an apple tree blooming amid the thickets....	Under the apple tree I awoke you....
His left hand under my head His right hand embraces me I beg of you swear it daughters of Jerusalem....	His left hand under my head His right had embraces me I beg of you, swear it, Daughters of Jerusalem....
NIGHT ONE **Ending**	NIGHT SEVEN **Beginning**

It is hard to look at these poems and deny that this ring structure was intentional.

Looking at one particular choice makes this more convincing. Remember that the final stanza of the poem (Night Seven) is a variation on a refrain that is used to end Nights Two and Three. Again, here's the end of Night Seven:

> Haste you away, lover...
> And be as a gazelle or a wild roe
> On all the mountains of spices...

Here's the end of Night Two:

> My lover is mine and I am my lover's!
> He grazes through the wild scarlet.
>
> Now, before the day breathes
> And the shadows flee,

> Turn from me and be, my lover,
> As a gazelle or a wild roe,
> On the cleft and jagged mountains.

And here is Night Three:

> *Now before the day breathes*
> *And the shadows flee,*
> *I will get me to the mountain of myrrh*
> *And to the hill of frankincense!*

Each represents the end of the night and the need for the lover to flee before the day comes. In Night Two the lover is asked to 'turn.' In Night Three the lover says "I will get me to..." But only in Night Seven is the word 'haste' used. There is only one other use of 'haste' in the Song of Songs and that is in the opening section of the poem. This variation of the refrain using this word cannot be accidental. By changing 'turn' to 'haste' in that last refrain, the text now satisfies the needs of both formal structures, both finishing the Night appropriately *and* forming the outermost ring of the poem. Choices like this one are made throughout the poem.

Night Three and Night Five form a clear second ring. I'm calling this the C ring. This time they are parallel poems rather than inverted poems.

Night Three	Night Five
I sought but found him not....	I sought but found him not....
I beg of you, swear it, Daughters of Jerusalem....	I beg of you, swear it, Daughters of Jerusalem....

Poem of praise for boy ending:	Poem of praise for boy ending:
Daughters of Jerusalem, come, arise. Feast your eyes, you Daughters of Zion. Gaze on my king, my Solomon....	This is my lover, This is my darling friend, Daughters of Jerusalem....
Poem of praise (wasf) for the girl:	Poem of praise (wasf) for the girl:
And your hair like goats, a coal-black flock, *Trailing down rugged Mount Gilead.* *Your teeth like a flock of the whitest sheep,* *smoothly shorn,* *Just rising from the washing pond,* *Bearing twins, each and all,* *Barren-wombed, none....*	*Your hair is like goats, a coal-black flock* *Trailing down rugged Mount Gilead.* *Your teeth like a flock of the whitest sheep,* *smoothly shorn,* *Just rising from the washing pond,* *Bearing twins, each and all,* *Barren-wombed none....*

This leaves us only with Night Two, Night Four, and Night Six.

Night Two and Six both have functions in my narrative understanding of the poem. Night Two establishes clearly the call-come-make love structure of the nights. Night Six is the bringing (either in fantasy or reality) of their love into the public eye. The praise that the boy had heaped on her is now given to her by the public. Other than this the two poems are not that similar and maybe it is a stretch to call them B and B'. They do, though, both end with a version of the same refrain.

Night Two Ending	Night Six Ending
"My lover is mine and I am my lover's! He grazes through the wild scarlet."	"Flowing to my lover smoothly, Flowing onto scarlet lips. I am my lover's and for me is his passion."

Again notice the variation in the refrain and what it might mean for the development of the relationship.

If the rings are as I suggest, the center of the poem is the beautiful Night Four: The Garden of Lebanon. This poem is composed of five sections. The third section, that is, the center section, and, therefore, the center of the entire Song of Songs is the following:

> A garden enclosed is my sister, my bride,
> A guarded pool enclosed, a sealed fountain,
> Your secluded springs are my refuge –
> Not only pomegranates, but all the choicest fruits,
> Not only henna, but nard,
> Not only nard and saffron, cane and cinnamon, but every
>   kind of incense tree,
> Not only myrrh and aloes, but each and all of the most exotic
>   spices –
> A garden fountain,
> A welling of living water,
> Cascades from Lebanon.

This passage begins with an unusual repetition, three different adjectives and nouns suggesting an enclosed place: "a garden enclosed," "A guarded pool enclosed," "A sealed fountain." Each of these also suggests a place of refuge and seclusion.

This to me is a spine-tingling example of form and content merging. Here at the center of the rings, at the center of the poem is a garden enclosed. Here at the center is the place of refuge, hidden, wall within wall within wall, within all the rings of A, and the B ring and the C ring and the four other poems of Night Four. Here in poem three of Night Four, we sit at the center of the circles, but we also sit at a pause in the cycles. It is a quiet place before the drama begins. Here before the dangers of Night Five, here before the "coming-out" party of Night Six, here before the growth and maturation of the girl in Night Seven, here at the very geometric center of the poem is "a refuge," "a garden enclosed," the girl herself, "a garden fountain," the very girl herself.

Note on the Translation

First, I must acknowledge my debt to the translations and scholarship of Chana and Ariel Block, Marvin H. Pope, Michael Fox and Wilfred G.E. Watson. The work they did exploring the possible meanings of every single word in the original text made my translation possible.

As I mentioned earlier, I began my work on the Song with an intent to study the chiastic structure of the poem. Whenever translating poetry, though, one is faced with a series of impossible tradeoffs. Do you translate only the literal meaning of the words? Do you do work to uncover and bring out the connotations of the words? Do you try to hold onto the rhythm, music, prosody of the original? Do you keep together the original formal structure of the poem?

Translating from one language to another is difficult enough in prose, but if you have to maintain all of the elements that are important to making a poem the poem it is, it becomes truly impossible. No word in one language is entirely translatable into a single word in another. At the very least, the sonic properties of the words will be different and, therefore, function differently within poetry. But each word also carries with it a host of connotations that are never the same from one language to the next.

My translation is most concerned with bringing out the resonances that would emphasize the overall structure of the poem. Where one word has two strong meanings, I might have used both in my translation so as not to lose important flavors or resonances with other parts of the poem. What this means is that the original music of the lines is lost several times in this translation.

I note two places where this trade-off is most obvious.

In the opening stanza, I have translated one word as both "name" and "soul." Both of these meanings are relevant and important both at that moment in the poem and in resonance with later elements in the poem. This leads to a very different rhythm then you find in other translations. I would argue that it is no less faithful to the original meaning and intent of the poem. Indeed, one might argue that by choosing one of the two words over the other, one is altering the poem more significantly than I do by leaving multiple obvious meanings in place.

Another difficult place was in the center poem The Garden of Lebanon:

> A garden enclosed is my sister, my bride,
> A guarded pool enclosed, a sealed fountain,
> Your secluded springs are my refuge.

"Your secluded springs are my refuge" is not a line that exists as is in the original. But the sense of refuge and seclusion is implicit in the language that describes the fountain and pool above. It seemed much more important to keep that sense available to an English reader (especially given this poem's structural location) than to maintain the appropriate number of lines or the rhythm of the original.

There are smaller similar choices made throughout. They are almost always choices made so as not to lose important meanings. Perhaps the chief poetic device in the Song is thematic and verbal resonance. The poem is constantly repeating itself cyclically, circularly. I felt it important above all not to hide any of that resonance. To me the poem is a hall of harmonious echoes. Literal word for word translation of the Song, therefore, can have the effect of putting your thumb on a ringing bell.

SONG OF SONGS

OF SOLOMON

PART I

Night One

I. Black and Lovely

i. haste me away with you

Girl:

>Let me drink the kisses of the king's mouth
>For your sweet loving outflows wine.
>It flows out, love, as the sweetest oils.
>Your name, your soul is a slow, sweet oil.
>And so all the women want you.
>
>Haste me away with you, my king,
>And bring me with you to the king's chambers.
>Let us exult in you, your soul, your name,
>And rejoice that your loving outflows wine.
>How smooth are they to want you.

ii. brothers and vineyards

Girl:

Yes, I am black and I am lovely, Daughters Of Jerusalem.
Black and lovely as the night nomads' goat-hair tents.
Lovely and black as the pavilions of Solomon.
So see me not only for my little black dawn.

I have burned in the glare of that sun.
Because my brothers were incensed with me
They made me keep their vineyards for them.
So my vineyard own I did not keep.

II. Meeting in the Cedars

i. tell me where

Girl:

"Tell me, my soul's chosen love,
Where will you desire to graze today?
Where will you lie your animals from out the midday sun?
Tell me where so that I am not seen wandering
Like a veiled woman through your companions' flocks."

Boy:

If, loveliest among women, you still choose not to know.
Then you should go ahead and wander
The tracks of the flocks.
Go graze your kids wherever you desire
And among the other shepherds' tents.

ii. indeed you are lovely

Boy:

> *I've dreamed of you, my darling,*
> *As a wild mare in the midst of Solomon's chariots.*
>
> *Your cheeks are beautiful bridled with bangles,*
> *Your neck is beautiful strung with slotted beads.*
> *Bangles of gold, we will make for you,*
> *Dotted with studs of silver.*

Girl:

> While my king reclined in the king's chambers
> My nard gave forth its fragrant spice.
>
> My lover is a sachet of myrrh
> That will lie all night between my breasts.
> My lover is a cluster of henna-roses
> From the gardens round the Fountain at En-Gedi.

Boy:

> *Indeed you are lovely, my darling.*
> *Indeed you are lovely.*
>
> *Your eyes are very doves.*

6

Girl:

Indeed you are lovely, my lover,
You are truly beautiful.

Our bed is lush.
The beams of our houses are the cedars.
The rafters of our houses are the junipers.

iii. a wild scarlet of the valley

Girl:

I am just a wild rose of the Sharon plain,
A wild scarlet of the valley.

Boy:

Like a scarlet blossoming through the thistle in the clefts
    of the cliff,
So is my darling among all women.

Girl:

Like the apple tree blooming amid the thickets in the wild
    wood,
So is my lover among all men.

And have I delighted in sitting in that shade.
The fruit has been sweet on my tongue.
He brought me beneath the cedars for feasting and wine
And he declared his desire for me.

Put me to bed among scarlet blossoms.
Spread me out amid the apples.
I am faint with desire.

His left hand under my head,
His right hand embraces me.

8

I beg of you, swear it, Daughters of Jerusalem,
By the gazelles and the does of the wild
Do not disturb, do not bestir[1] our loving
Until our love is satisfied.

---

[1] "Do not disturb, do not bestir." I found this in Michael V. Fox's translation and could not improve it.

Night Two
My Lover Calls

i. my lover comes

Girl:

Hark! Hear my lover.
Look! See he comes now.

Leaping over mountains
Bounding over hills
My lover like the beautiful gazelle, the young wild roe.

Now he stands at our back wall,
Gazing in the stone windows,
Peering through the cracks in the rock.

ii. my lover calls

Girl:

My lover spoke to me and said:

Boy:

Come arise, my darling.
My lovely one, come away.

The season of cold rains is passed.
The heavy storms are finished, gone away.

Again the sight of blossoms on the earth,
The season of pruning and singing,
Again the voices of turtledoves across our land.

The fig tree sweetens its budding fruits,
And the blooming fruit of the vine gives off its fragrance.

Come arise, my darling.
My lovely one, come away.

My dove in the clefts of the cliff,
In the coverts of the rock,

Let me see your face.

Let me hear your voice.
For your voice is delicious.
And your face is lovely.

ii. brothers and vineyards

Brothers:

> Catch us the foxes!
> The little foxes!
> The vineyard spoilers!
> Our vineyards are in bloom.

iv. my lover is mine

Girl:

My lover is mine and I am my lover's!
He grazes through the wild scarlet.

Now, before the day breathes
And the shadows flee,
Turn from me and be, my lover,
As a gazelle or a wild roe,
On the cleft and jagged mountains.

Night Three

I. I Sought my Soul's Chosen

Girl:

Then night followed night in our bed,

      And I sought my soul's chosen love.
I sought but found him not.

"I will rise and round the city!
      I will seek my soul's chosen!"

I sought but found him not.
They found me then, the watchmen round the city.

"My soul's chosen –
Have you seen him?"
And scarcely had I passed them
When I found him, my soul's chosen love.

I caught him to me and would not let him go
Until I'd brought him to my mother's house,
To the chambers of she who bore me.

I beg of you, swear it, Daughters of Jerusalem,
By the gazelles and the does of the wild
Do not disturb, do not bestir our loving

Until our love is satisfied.

Daughters:
> Who is she, that dawn rising
> From the wild steppe
> Like a pillar of smoke,
> Smoldering with the fragrance of myrrh and
>> frankincense,
> With smoke from all the traders' fragrant powders?

II. Banter

Girl:

Look! It is my king's, my Solomon's bed, his own.
Defended by threescore warriors
The bravest of all the warriors of Israel,
War-trained, battle-tested,
Each with sword a-thigh
Against all dread that might disturb our night!

A throne-bed for himself has made my king,
My Solomon, from the wood of Lebanon.
The columns he made of silver,
The bolster-spread of gold.
The pillows were of purple wool.
The chamber walls inlaid with colored stones.

Daughters of Jerusalem, come, arise.
Feast your eyes, you Daughters of Zion.
Gaze on my king, my Solomon
Gaze on the wreath his mother gives him
On this his wedding day,
This the day for the delighting of his heart!

III. Her First Wasf

Boy:

Indeed you are lovely, my darling.
Indeed you are lovely.
Your eyes are very doves
From within the veil of your tresses.
And your hair like goats, a coal-black flock,
Trailing down rugged Mount Gilead.
Your teeth like a flock of the whitest sheep, smoothly
        shorn,
Just rising from the washing pond,
Bearing twins, each and all,
Barren-wombed, none.

Like a thread of scarlet are your lips.
Your mouth is delicious.
Like the blush of pomegranate is your cheek
From within the veil of your tresses.

And your neck is like the tower of David
Erect in its perfection,
A necklace of a thousand shields hangs there –
One thousand bucklers, each from a true warrior.

And your breasts like two fawns,
Twins from a gazelle,

20

Grazing through the wild scarlet.

Now before the day breathes
And the shadows flee,
I will get me to the mountain of myrrh
And to the hill of frankincense!

You are entirely beautiful, my darling,
You are wholly without blemish.

Night Four
Garden of Lebanon

i. come, my bride

Boy:

From the ranges of Lebanon, bride,
From the ranges of Lebanon, come.
Descend from the peak of Amana
From the peaks of Senir and Hermon,
From out the lions' dens,
From out the leopards' lairs.

ii. you have abducted my heart

Boy:

>You have abducted my heart, my sister, my bride.
>You have abducted my heart with a single gleam from your
>>eye,
>With a single gleaming gem from your necklace.
>
>How sweet your loving, my sister,
>Your loving outflows any wine.
>The simplest oils of your soul flow sweeter than any spice.
>From your lips, my bride, drops honey.
>Molasses and milk pool under your tongue.
>The fragrance of your dress is the very fragrance of
>>Lebanon.

iii. a garden enclosed

Boy:

A garden enclosed is my sister, my bride,
A guarded pool enclosed, a sealed fountain,
Your secluded springs are my refuge –
Not only pomegranates, but all the choicest fruits,
Not only henna, but nard,
Not only nard and saffron, cane and cinnamon, but every
*   kind of incense tree,*
Not only myrrh and aloes, but each and all of the most
*   exotic spices –*
A garden fountain,
A welling of living water,
Cascades from Lebanon.

iv. breathe breath into my garden

Girl:

> Stir north-wind!
> Come, enter, south!
> Breathe breath into my garden
> That its spices may flow and blow about.
> Let my lover come into his garden!
> Let him eat of the choicest fruits!

v. i have come into my garden

Boy:

I have come into my garden, my sister, my bride.
Not only have I gathered my myrrh, but also my spice.
Not only have I eaten my honeycomb, but also my honey.
Not only have I drunk my wine, but also my milk.

> *"Eat well, friends, drink yourselves drunk on*
> *loving!"*

PART II

Night Five

I. My Lover Calls and I Sought My Soul's Chosen

Girl:

I, I slept, but my heart was disturbed.
Hark! Hear my lover entreating me:

Boy:

Open to me, my sister, my darling,
My dove, my perfect one.
For my head is drenched with dew,
My curls with the misting night.

Girl:

"I have removed my robes,
Must I put them on again, my king?
I have cleansed the soft of my feet.
Must I soil them again, my king?"

The hard of his hand through the hole
in the door thrust my love.
My innermost loins moved at his cause.
I, I rose to open and yield to my lover.
My hands dripped myrrh,
My fingers liquid myrrh
Onto the handle of the bolt.
I, I opened to my lover,

But he'd turned and fled.
My very soul nearly failed at his flight.

I sought but found him not.
I called but he answered not.

They found me then, the watchmen round the city.
They beat me, bruised me,
Lifted from me my scarves,
Those men who watch the walls.

I beg of you to swear it, Daughters of Jerusalem,
If you find my lover, what will you tell him?
Do not tell him I am faint with desire.

Daughters:

> What is your lover from all other lovers
> O loveliest among women?
> What is your lover from all other lovers
> That we must promise you?

Girl:

> My lover is white with light, red with manhood,
> The highest of a myriad.
> His head is gold, is gold.
> His curls, hill upon hill,
> Black as raven.

> His eyes are like doves by the springs,
> Bathed in milk as they sit by the brimming pools.
> His face sweet like a bed of spices,
> A burgeoning of mixed scents.

> Wild scarlets his lips,
> Dripping liquid myrrh.

Rods of gold his arms to the hand,
Studded with stones from Tarsheesh.
A block of ivory his loins,
Inlaid with lapis lazuli.
Alabaster pillars his legs from the thigh,
Set on pedestals of gold, of gold.

His soul is like glorious Lebanon
Exalted as the cedars.
His words are sweet wine.
He is entirely desirable.

This is my lover,
This is my darling friend,
Daughters of Jerusalem.

Daughters:

> Where has your lover gone
> O loveliest among women?
> Where has your lover turned?
> That we may help you find him.

Girl:

My lover has come down to his garden
To the beds of spices.
He will graze in the garden
and gather the wild scarlet.
I am my lover's and my lover is mine!
He grazes through the wild scarlet.

II. Her Second Wasf

Boy:

You are lovely, my darling, as Tirzah in the north
As beautiful in the south as Jerusalem.
But terrible and bright as the most high.
Turn your eyes from me,
For they disturb me –
Your hair is like goats, a coal-black flock,
Trailing down rugged Mount Gilead.
Your teeth like a flock of the whitest sheep, smoothly
        shorn,
Just rising from the washing pond,
Bearing twins, each and all,
Barren-wombed, none.
Like the blush of pomegranate is your cheek
From within the veil of your tresses –

Threescore queens may there be,
Fourscore concubines
And women without number.
But one is she always, my dove, my undefiled,
One is she. To her mother,
Without blemish is she. To her who bore her.
The young women saw her and praised her.
Queens and concubines sang her lauds:

Daughters:

"Who is she – that dawn rising?
Lovely as the moon
Flawless as the sun
Terrible and bright as the most high?"

Boy:

I'd come to the garden of walnut trees
To look on the lush of the rushes beside the cascades.
To see if the fruit on the vines were budding.
To see if the pomegranate trees were in blossom.

Girl:

Before I was aware, my soul's desire had set me,
On the pillowed throne-bed with my prince.

Night Six
Turn! Turn!

His Companions:

    Turn, turn back, O flawless one, Shulammite!
    Turn, turn back, that we may study you!

Girl:

    Study not the flawless one, the Shulammite,
    As if she were a veiled camp-dancer.

His Companions:

    How sweet your sandaled steps,
    O princely daughter.
    The turns of your thighs like jewels
    Worked by the hard of artists' hands.
    Your navel a well-turned goblet,
    May it never lack for wines.
    Your belly a mound of wheat
    Hedged-in with wild scarlet.
    And your breasts like two fawns,
    Twins from a gazelle.
    Your neck like an ivory tower
    Erect in its perfection.
    Your eyes, daughter, the pools of Heshbon,

At the gate of your princely city,
Your nose like the tower of Lebanon
Facing Damascus,
On you, your head like the crimson Mount Carmel
And the threads on your head like blue-black
      purple,
A king is caught in that streaming.
How beautiful, how pleasant, you are, love,
O delightful daughter.

Boy:

Your bearing resembled a palm tree,
Your breasts clusters of dates.
I said to myself, "I will climb this palm
I will take hold of its high-branched fruit."
May your breasts be like clusters on the vine
The scent of your breath like apples
And your mouth like the best wine –

Girl:

Flowing to my lover smoothly,
Flowing onto scarlet lips.
I am my lover's and for me is his passion.

Night Seven

I. I Call My Lover

i. come, lover

Girl:

Come, lover, let's to the fields
Let's lie all night among the henna
Let's be off early to the vineyards
To see if the fruit of the vines has budded
If the blooms have opened
If the pomegranate trees are in blossom
There, I will give you my loving.
There, the love-mandrake gives off its fragrant spice.
At our thresholds wait all manner of delicious fruit,
Fruit both new to us and old.
My loving, for you, I have saved.

ii. who is that dawn rising?

Girl:

O, if only you were my brother,
Who had nursed at the breasts of my mother.
Then when I'd seek your lips in the streets,
I would sip your kisses there,
And no one would despise me for it.
I would lead you, take you
To my mother's house
To the chambers of she who bore me.
I would give you spiced wine to sip,
The juice of my pomegranate.

His left hand under my head,
His right hand embraces me

I beg of you, swear it, Daughters of Jerusalem,
Do not ever disturb, do not ever bestir our loving
Until our love is satisfied.

Daughters:

Who is she that dawn rising
from the wild steppe
clinging to her lover?

iii. fierce as death is love

Girl:

Under the apple tree I awoke you,
There where your mother conceived you,
There where she gave birth to you.

Set me as a signet over your heart
As a signet over the hard of your hand.
For fierce as death is love,
As sure as the tomb its envy.
Its wounds are wounds of fire,
Wounds of conflagration.
Mighty floods could never quench love,
No torrent could ever wash it away.

Should a man give all his wealth for love,
Surely, the world would despise him for it.

II. My Vineyard Own

i. brothers

Brothers:

We have a younger sister
Whose breasts are yet to come.
What to do for our sister
When she is spoken for?

If she be a wall,
We will build upon her silver turrets
But if she be a door,
We will barricade her with cedar.

Girl:

I am a wall —
　　And my breasts are already towers!
And thus in his eye
　　Already am I a fountain of joy.

ii. vineyards

Girl:

Solomon had a vineyard in Bal Hamon, the Fertile Hill.
      He gave the vineyard unto keepers.
      Each could earn for its fruit a thousand silver pieces.

My vineyard own I keep before me now.
      Let Solomon have his thousand pieces,
      The keepers of the fruit their two hundred.

iii. haste you away

Boy:

O garden-dweller –
My companions attend to you –
But let it be me that hears your voice –

Girl:

Haste you away, lover...
And be as a gazelle or a wild roe
On all the mountains of spices...

Bibliography

Bloch, Chana and Ariel. **The Song of Songs.** Modern Library (Oct 10 2006).

Carr, Lloyd. **The Song of Solomon: An Introduction and Commentary.** Inter-Varsity Press. 1984.

Davidson, Richard M. "The Literary Structure of the Song of Songs *Redivivus." Journal of the Adventist Theological Society 14/2 (FALL 2003): 44-65.*

Exum, J. Cheryl. "A Literary and Structural Analysis of the Song of Songs." **ZAW** 85 (1973): 47-79.

Fox, Michael V. **The Song of Songs and the Ancient Egyptian Love Songs.** University of Wisconsin Press. 1985.

Pope, Marvin H. **Songs of Songs: A New Translation with Introduction and Commentary (Anchor Bible).** Doubleday. 1977.

Shea, William H. "The Chiastic Structure of the Song of Songs" **Alttestamentliche Wissenschaft** 92, 1980, pages 378-96.

Watson, Wilfred G.E. **Classical Hebrew Poetry: A Guide to its Techniques (The Library of Hebrew Bible/Old Testament Studies).** Bloomsbury T&T Clark; 1 edition (November 1, 2009)

Webster, Edwin C. "Pattern in the Song of Songs." **JSOT** 22 (1982) 73-93.

www.ingramcontent.com/pod-product-compliance
Lightning Source LLC
Chambersburg PA
CBHW021939040426
42448CB00008B/1149